Mastering Mojo

High Performance Programming

for AI Applications

Benson Paul

Table of Contents

Chapter One

Introduction to Mojo Programming

The Origins and Purpose of Mojo

In the fast-evolving world of AI, speed is everything. Whether you're crunching massive data sets, training neural networks, or deploying models at scale, performance isn't a luxury—it's a necessity. That's exactly why **Mojo** was born.

Developed by **Modular AI**, Mojo aims to solve one of the biggest tensions in modern programming: the tradeoff between developer productivity and raw system performance. For years, data scientists and AI engineers have relied on Python for its simplicity and vast ecosystem. But as models grew larger and demands got tougher, Python's performance limitations began to show.

Mojo offers a fresh solution. It combines Python's familiar syntax with the high-performance capabilities of systems languages like C++ and Rust. In essence, Mojo was built to **bring performance**

and simplicity under one roof—a single language that feels like Python but performs like C.

Imagine writing code that's as expressive and readable as Python, yet runs fast enough to replace C++ in critical workloads. That's the promise of Mojo—and it's already changing the game in AI tooling.

Mojo vs Python, Rust, and C++

To truly appreciate Mojo, it helps to see how it compares with the giants it's trying to unify or outpace:

Feature	Mojo	Python	Rust	C++
Perform ance	Near C-level (via static types)	Slower, dynamic	Very fast	Very fast
Ease of Use	High (Python-lik e syntax)	Very high	Mediu m (steep learni ng	Medi um

	Mojo	Python	Rust	C++
			curve)	
Memory Safety	Strong (optional ownership)	Weak (GC + leaks)	Very strong	Manual
AI/ML Ecosystem	Emerging (Python interop)	Massive	Growing	Limited
Concurrency	Task-based & efficient	Threading/GIL	Advanced (async)	Low-level threads
Best Use Case	AI, ML, High-performance compute	Data Science	Systems, Web	Games, Systems

Python remains king in accessibility and libraries, but Mojo addresses the Achilles' heel: performance. **Rust** excels in memory safety and zero-cost abstractions but is complex. **C++** gives you raw power—but at the cost of manual memory management and verbosity. Mojo, in contrast, aims to give you the *best of all worlds*.

Installing and Setting Up Mojo

Step 1: Sign Up for Modular

Mojo is currently accessible through the **Modular platform**, which includes an online environment and CLI tools. Head over to https://www.modular.com/mojo and create an account.

Step 2: Access the Playground (Optional)

Modular offers an online playground—no installation needed. It's perfect for quick experimentation:

- Visit: https://www.modular.com/play
- Start typing Mojo code directly in your browser.

Step 3: Install Mojo CLI (If Available for Your OS)

If local installation is supported for your platform:

```
curl -L https://get.modular.com |
bash
```

Then follow the prompts to install the Modular CLI, including Mojo.

Note: As of early 2025, Mojo is still under development, so full access may be limited or evolving. Stay updated through Modular's blog.

Your First Mojo Program

Let's get our hands dirty. Here's a simple Mojo program to print "Hello, AI World!" and understand the syntax:

```
fn main():
    print("Hello, AI World!")
```

What Just Happened?

- `fn main():` is the function declaration syntax. Mojo uses `fn` instead of Python's `def`.
- `print()` behaves just like Python. If you know Python, Mojo feels very familiar.

Let's add a bit more:

```
fn add(x: Int, y: Int) -> Int:
    return x + y
fn main():
    let result = add(5, 3)
    print("5 + 3 =", result)
```

Key Mojo Features in This Snippet:

- **Static Types**: `x: Int` and `y: Int` are statically typed. You can also omit types for dynamic inference.
- **Return Type**: `-> Int` explicitly shows the function returns an integer.
- **Let vs Var**: Mojo distinguishes between `let` (immutable) and `var` (mutable) just like Swift or Rust.

Chapter Two

Mojo Fundamentals

Variables and Data Types

In Mojo, variables are the building blocks of every program, and the language encourages clear thinking about how data is stored, accessed, and modified.

Immutable vs Mutable Variables

Mojo introduces two kinds of variable bindings:

- `let` for **immutable** (read-only) variables.
- `var` for **mutable** (changeable) variables.

Example:
```
let name = "Mojo"
var count = 3
```
Here, `name` can't be reassigned—trying to do so would throw a compile-time error. On the other hand, `count` can be updated.
```
count = count + 1
```

Why does this matter? Immutability leads to safer, more predictable code—especially in concurrent environments. Mojo encourages immutability by default, much like Rust or Swift.

Data Types in Mojo

Mojo supports both **dynamic** and **static** typing, allowing you to prototype quickly or optimize for performance.

Basic Types:

- `Int`: Integer values
- `Float`: Floating point numbers
- `Bool`: Boolean (true/false)
- `String`: Text data

Example:

```
let age: Int = 30
let pi: Float = 3.14
let is_ready: Bool = true
let greeting: String = "Hello, Mojo!"
```

Notice the **type annotations**. Mojo infers types when you omit them, but you can specify them for clarity or performance.

Custom Structs

Mojo supports defining your own data structures using `struct`:

```
struct Person:
    var name: String
    var age: Int
```

This is similar to classes in Python, but without the overhead. Mojo structs are lean and memory-efficient, making them ideal for high-performance scenarios.

Functions and Control Flow

Functions in Mojo are first-class citizens—they're easy to declare, support type annotations, and can be composed cleanly.

Declaring Functions

```
fn greet(name: String) -> String:
```

```
    return "Hello, " + name
```

This function takes a string and returns another. Mojo supports both **explicit return types** and **type inference**.

You can also write a more concise version:

```
fn greet(name):
    return "Hello, " + name
```

This works fine for simple scripts, especially when prototyping.

Conditionals

Mojo's `if` statements are similar to Python, but they enforce parentheses around conditions for clarity:

```
fn classify_temperature(temp: Int):
    if (temp < 0):
        print("Freezing")
    elif (temp < 20):
        print("Cold")
    else:
        print("Warm")
```

Loops

For Loops:

```
for i in range(0, 5):
    print("Count:", i)
```

Mojo's `range()` is zero-based and exclusive of the upper limit, just like in Python.

While Loops:

```
var count = 0
while (count < 3):
    print("Still counting:", count)
    count = count + 1
```

Pattern Matching (Preview Feature)

Although still experimental, Mojo is working toward powerful **pattern matching** akin to Rust and Swift. It allows expressive branching logic with clean syntax, especially useful for handling enums or complex state flows.

Tuples: Lightweight Data Grouping

Tuples in Mojo let you group values without creating a named structure. They're great for quick data passing or returning multiple values from a function.

Basic Tuple Example:

```
let point = (10, 20)
print("X:", point.0)
print("Y:", point.1)
```

Mojo allows tuple *destructuring* too:

```
let (x, y) = point
print("Coordinates:", x, y)
```

Tuples are immutable by default and are ideal for simple, temporary groupings.

Structs: Organized and Efficient Custom Types

Structs are Mojo's version of classes—but slimmer, safer, and built for performance.

Declaring a Struct:

```
struct Vector2D:
    var x: Float
    var y: Float
```

```
fn magnitude(v: Vector2D) -> Float:
    return (v.x * v.x + v.y *
v.y).sqrt()
```

Structs can include default values, computed methods (coming soon), and are stack-allocated by default—meaning they don't suffer from the dynamic memory overhead Python objects often do.

Creating and Using Structs:

```
let v = Vector2D(x=3.0, y=4.0)
print("Length:", magnitude(v))
```

This creates a 2D vector and computes its length using the Pythagorean theorem. With types like this, AI algorithms—especially those involving tensors and vectors—become much more efficient.

Enums: Defining Explicit Choices

Enums are perfect when you want to model a value that can only be *one of several predefined states*. This is especially useful in AI systems for things like model states, layer types, or activation functions.

Basic Enum Example:

```
enum Activation:
    RELU
    SIGMOID
    TANH
```

You can use them in match-style conditionals:

```
fn describe(act: Activation):
    if (act == Activation.RELU):
        print("Fast    and    sparse
activation")
    elif (act ==
Activation.SIGMOID):
        print("Smooth and
probabilistic")
    elif (act == Activation.TANH):
        print("Centered        and
smooth")
```

Modules and Imports

As your Mojo programs grow in complexity, organization becomes key. Mojo supports **modules** and **imports**, allowing you to break code into reusable files and libraries—just like in Python, but without dynamic loading issues.

Creating a Module:

Let's say you've created a file called `math_utils.mojo`:

```
# math_utils.mojo
fn square(x: Int) -> Int:
    return x * x
```

In your main script, you can import and use it:

```
import math_utils
fn main():
    print("4 squared is",
math_utils.square(4))
```

Modules make it easy to organize your AI projects into components—think layers, datasets, training loops—all modular and optimized.

Aliasing Imports:

You can use aliases to keep things short:

```
import math_utils as mu
print(mu.square(9))
```

Chapter Three

Mojo's Type System

Why Type Systems Matter

In AI and high-performance computing, types aren't just for clarity—they're the backbone of optimization. The difference between runtime inference and compile-time certainty can mean the difference between hours and milliseconds.

Mojo recognizes this and gives you the best of both worlds: **dynamic typing when you want speed of development**, and **static typing when you want speed of execution**.

Static vs Dynamic Typing in Mojo

Most people coming from Python are used to dynamic typing—you just declare a variable and it figures things out:

```
x = 42
x = "forty-two"  # This is fine in
Python
```

This version is more flexible and still works—but may be slower and less predictable at compile time. Use this during prototyping, then tighten up types for performance.

Why Static Types Matter for AI

Let's say you're implementing a tensor operation, like dot product:

```
fn dot(a: [Float], b: [Float]) ->
Float:
    var result: Float = 0.0
    for i in range(0, len(a)):
        result += a[i] * b[i]
    return result
```

With **static arrays and floats**, Mojo can:

- Inline operations
- Eliminate dynamic bounds checking
- Vectorize instructions at compile time

This is the kind of performance boost that really matters in deep learning pipelines.

Custom Types and Generics (Preview)

Mojo is evolving toward more advanced typing features, like:

- **Generic functions** (e.g., `fn identity[T](x: T) -> T`)
- **Custom traits/interfaces** for enforcing contracts
- **Dependent types** and **shape-based types** for tensors

These features will make Mojo capable of expressing tensor dimensions, layer shapes, and matrix compatibilities at compile time—not runtime. That's a revolution for AI devs.

Inference and Safety

One of Mojo's strengths is how it balances **developer ergonomics** with **compiler-level intelligence**. Type inference in Mojo means you don't *have* to write types everywhere—but when you do, the compiler rewards you with speed and safety.

Type Inference

You can write clean, readable code without constantly specifying types:

```
let temperature = 98.6   # Inferred as
Float
let is_valid = true      # Inferred as
Bool
```

Mojo uses **contextual inference**—meaning it often guesses the type based on how the value is used.

But if you're doing something ambiguous, Mojo will require clarification:

```
let value = None  # Error: Mojo
doesn't know what type 'value' should
be
```

In this case, you'd need to be explicit:

```
let value: Optional[Int] = None
```

This is how Mojo protects you from type ambiguity while keeping your code expressive and fast.

Safe by Design

Mojo is intentionally **safe by default**, which means:

- No implicit conversions that could lose data
- No null-pointer-style crashes
- No dynamic surprises at runtime if you've declared your types

Example: if you try to assign a `Float` to an `Int`, Mojo won't let it slide:

```
let a: Int = 3.14  # Compile-time
error
```

This type safety is especially important in AI applications where precision and edge cases matter.

Nullable Types and Optionals

In Python, you're used to using None everywhere. In Mojo, this idea still exists—but it's **explicit** and **type-safe** through the use of **Optional**.

What Are Optional

An Optional[T] is a type that might contain a value of type T, or it might contain None.

```
let maybe_score: Optional[Int] =
None
maybe_score = 95
```

This is great when you're dealing with:

- Missing data
- Optional config settings
- Results that might fail

Working with Optionals

Mojo encourages you to check if a value is present before using it. You do this with an **if let** style pattern:

```
let maybe_name: Optional[String] =
"Alice"
if (maybe_name is not None):
    print("User:", maybe_name!)
```

Notice the ! —this is the **unwrap operator**. It says: "I'm sure this is not None."

If you use ! without checking first, Mojo will error:

```
let maybe_id: Optional[Int] = None
print(maybe_id!)   # Runtime error or
compile-time warning
```

This protects you from NoneType crashes—common bugs in Python, JavaScript, and even Swift when handled sloppily.

Defaulting Optionals

Mojo allows default values using the or operator:

```
let display_name = maybe_name or
"Guest"
```

Chapter Four

Working with Collections

Collections are at the heart of any meaningful program. Whether you're processing training samples, transforming datasets, or aggregating results—Mojo gives you tools to do it fast, cleanly, and safely.

In this chapter, we'll look at:

- Lists
- Sets
- Maps
- Iterators
- Generators
- Functional tools like `map`, `filter`, and `reduce`

Lists

Lists in Mojo are ordered collections that grow and shrink dynamically, like Python's `list`, but they're implemented to be much faster and more type-safe.

Creating a List:

```
var numbers: List[Int] = [1, 2, 3, 4]
numbers.append(5)
print(numbers)   # [1, 2, 3, 4, 5]
```

List Access and Modification:

```
let first = numbers[0]
numbers[1] = 10
```

Mojo enforces bounds safety and type correctness, so you're not silently writing invalid code.

Sets

Sets are unordered collections of unique items. They're ideal for deduplication or fast membership testing.

Basic Set Example:

```
var fruits: Set[String] = Set()
fruits.add("apple")
```

```
fruits.add("banana")
fruits.add("apple")   # No
duplicates
print(fruits)   # {'apple',
'banana'}
```

Use sets when you care about presence, not order or duplicates—very common in AI for feature tracking, categories, etc.

Maps (aka Dictionaries)

Maps associate keys with values. They're one of the most powerful tools in any language—especially useful when dealing with configs, indexes, and structured records.

Declaring a Map:

```
var user_ages: Dict[String, Int] = {
    "Alice": 30,
    "Bob": 25
}
user_ages["Carol"] = 35
print(user_ages["Alice"])   # 30
```

Safe Key Lookup:

```
if ("Dave" in user_ages):
    print(user_ages["Dave"])
else:
    print("Not found")
```

Mojo's `Dict` behaves like Python's `dict`, but can be made strictly typed and compiled for better speed.

Iterators and Generators

In large-scale data work, laziness (in a good way) is key. Iterators and generators let you **process data on-demand**, rather than loading it all at once.

Iterators

Mojo lets you iterate over any iterable, like lists:

```
for n in numbers:
    print(n)
```

You can also create **custom iterators** using `iter` and `next`, though Mojo's generator model is often more ergonomic.

Generators

Generators produce values on demand—useful when you're dealing with large data streams.

Simple Generator Example:

```
fn countdown(n: Int) ->
Generator[Int]:
    while n > 0:
        yield n
        n -= 1
for val in countdown(5):
    print(val)
```

This will print 5 down to 1, without allocating a whole list in memory. That's huge for memory efficiency in model training, stream processing, or simulation tasks.

Functional Programming Techniques

Mojo also supports **functional tools** like map, filter, and reduce—perfect for clean, high-level logic.

map

```
let doubled = map(fn(x): x * 2, [1,
2, 3])   # [2, 4, 6]
```

filter

```
let evens = filter(fn(x): x % 2 == 0,
[1, 2, 3, 4])   # [2, 4]
```

reduce

```
let total = reduce(fn(a, b): a + b,
[1, 2, 3, 4])   # 10
```

These functions are especially powerful when pipelining AI datasets, transforming tensors, or composing pre-processing steps.

Chapter Five

Memory Management and Performance

When building high-performance operationg systems for AI application especially in AI—you can't ignore memory. Every byte counts. Every copy matters. Mojo was built for this world. In fact, Mojo gives you *the kind of control over memory you usually only get in C++ or Rust*—but with syntax and safety closer to Python.

This chapter will unpack:

- How memory works in Mojo
- Reference vs value semantics
- How to optimize performance with ownership and mutability in mind

Memory Models in Mojo

Unlike Python, which abstracts memory management behind automatic reference counting and garbage collection, Mojo is **low-level aware**—but not low-level painful.

You can choose to:

- Let Mojo manage memory like Python (easy mode)
- Or take control for raw speed (pro mode)

Mojo gives you:

- **Stack-based values** for speed
- **Heap-based references** for flexibility
- **Explicit ownership** for predictability

Stack vs Heap

Let's say you create a number:

```
let x: Int = 42
```

This is a stack-allocated integer. It's fast, lives in the function's frame, and disappears when the function ends. Think: no GC, no indirection, no overhead.

But if you want to store a list of user data that grows dynamically?

```
var users: List[String] = []
```

That's heap-allocated—because it grows, shrinks, and gets passed around.

In performance-heavy code, **knowing what lives where** is the difference between real-time processing and bottlenecks.

Reference vs Value Semantics

Let's get into a major distinction Mojo supports explicitly: **value semantics** vs **reference semantics**.

Value Semantics

This means **a copy is made** when you assign or pass a variable.

```
let a = 10
let b = a  # b is a copy of a
```

For primitives and small structs, this is fast and makes bugs easier to avoid. It's like passing by value in C++ or Swift.

Reference Semantics

Used for more complex objects, especially when mutability is needed.

```
var list_a: List[Int] = [1, 2, 3]
```

```
var list_b = list_a  # Reference, not
a copy
list_b.append(4)
print(list_a)  # [1, 2, 3, 4]
```

By default, Mojo's **containers behave like Python**—they're reference types. But you can write your own data types with value semantics if needed.

Mutability and Performance

Mojo enforces **explicit mutability**, which helps with optimization and safety. If a function changes its argument, it must be marked as `var`.

```
fn increment(var x: Int):
    x += 1
```

If you try to mutate a value without declaring it as `var`, Mojo will prevent it—this reduces accidental side-effects and makes the optimizer's job easier.

Borrowing and Copying

Mojo is expected to evolve with more **borrow-checking and ownership semantics** similar to Rust, but for now, the important idea is:

- **Copy when needed**
- **Reference when shared**
- **Borrow when temporary**

That mental model will keep your performance up and your bugs down.

A Practical Example: Tensor Copy vs Reference

Let's say you're working with a tensor:

```
var a: Tensor = get_tensor()
var b = a  # Reference (shared buffer)
```

Now, if b modifies the tensor, a will reflect that change.

If you want an actual copy (like for augmentation or independent batch ops):

```
var b = a.copy()
```

This forces a deep copy—more memory, but no shared mutation. Mojo makes you think about this, which is good.

Stack and Heap Management

In performance-sensitive programming, *where* your data lives is just as important as *how* you use it. Mojo exposes a memory model that gives you both **predictability** and **control**, reminiscent of C++, but safer and more expressive.

What Goes on the Stack?

- Primitive types (`Int`, `Float`, `Bool`)
- Small structs with value semantics
- Local variables with known size at compile-time

Why the stack?

- Fast allocation and deallocation (just move the stack pointer)
- Data is stored contiguously, which improves cache performance

- No garbage collection overhead

```
fn calc():
    let x: Int = 10 # Stack
allocated
    let y: Float = 20.5
    let z = x + y
```

What Goes on the Heap?

- Dynamically-sized collections (`List`, `Dict`, `Set`)
- Objects with internal mutability
- Anything shared between scopes or passed around by reference

Why the heap?

- Flexible size and lifetime
- Allows references and sharing
- Required for polymorphic or recursive data structures

```
fn build_list() -> List[Int]:
    var nums: List[Int] = [1, 2, 3]
```

```
nums.append(4)
return nums
```

Here, nums lives on the heap and persists outside the function scope.

Performance Implications

- **Stack is fast but limited**: Use it for short-lived, simple data
- **Heap is flexible but slower**: Use when your data lives beyond the current scope or grows dynamically

💡 *Rule of thumb*: Favor stack for tight loops and small math-heavy routines. Use heap for user data, graphs, tensors, and ML batches.

Debugging and Profiling Tools

No matter how elegant your code is, you'll hit issues—bugs, memory leaks, slowdowns. Mojo is still early-stage, but it's designed with visibility in mind.

1. Compile-Time Checks

Mojo catches many issues before runtime:

- Type mismatches
- Invalid references
- Immutable mutation
- Buffer overflows (planned)

This eliminates entire classes of bugs you'd have to chase down in Python.

2. Runtime Debug Output

You can always fall back to classic techniques:

```
print("Shape      of      tensor:      ",
tensor.shape)
```

This works because Mojo supports Pythonic string formatting and introspection.

3. Profiling Performance

As of now, Mojo is building native integration with LLVM-based tools like:

- `perf` (on Linux)
- `Instruments` (on macOS)

- `valgrind` and `massif` for heap analysis

And soon:

- **Mojo-native profiling hooks** to measure execution time and memory usage block-by-block.

For now, you can annotate code manually:

```
let start = now()
run_model()
let end = now()
print("Execution time: ", end - start)
```

4. Integration with Python Debuggers

Because Mojo can call and be called from Python (via `pyimport` and `pyexport`), you can also:

- Use `pdb` to debug high-level logic
- Use `cProfile` on mixed Mojo+Python projects
- Inspect heap and stack with Python-side tools

Chapter Six

Parallelism and Concurrency

In modern computing, performance is all about **doing more in less time**. Mojo's parallelism and concurrency model is designed to make it easy to take full advantage of multicore processors and parallel hardware. Whether you're distributing tensor operations or handling multiple tasks at once, Mojo's model ensures that you're not just running code—you're running it **efficiently**.

This chapter will cover:

- Mojo's approach to **parallel execution**
- Understanding **threads**, **tasks**, and **futures**
- Optimizing parallel execution in Mojo

Mojo' s Parallel Execution Model

Mojo is designed to run tasks in parallel, across multiple CPU cores or even across different machines when needed. At the heart of Mojo's execution model is a **task-based** approach, where you define **tasks** to run in parallel, and Mojo handles distributing those tasks across the available threads efficiently.

Parallelism via Tasks

A *task* in Mojo is essentially a unit of work that can be run concurrently. Mojo's runtime scheduler ensures that tasks are distributed to threads efficiently, taking advantage of all available cores. Here's a quick example of creating a parallel task:

```
fn        process_data_parallel(data:
List[Int]) -> List[Int]:
    return parallel_map(data, fn(x):
x * 2)  # Multiplies all items by 2 in
parallel
```

Here, `parallel_map` automatically runs the function across multiple threads, giving you a concurrent execution pattern that is easy to scale without worrying about the intricacies of thread management.

Threads, Tasks, and Futures

In Mojo, the basic building blocks for concurrency are **threads**, **tasks**, and **futures**. Understanding each is key to writing efficient, performant code.

Threads

A **thread** is the smallest unit of execution. Mojo manages threads automatically under the hood, ensuring that tasks are distributed across them as needed. You won't manually create and manage threads like in C++ or Rust; instead, Mojo abstracts away this complexity by providing high-level tools like tasks and futures.

Tasks

A **task** represents a unit of work that Mojo can execute concurrently. Tasks can be used for anything from a lightweight operation to more complex logic that requires parallel execution.

```
var result = task(fn(): Int:
    // Task logic here
    return 42
```

)

The task is executed concurrently with the rest of your program. Mojo's scheduler will figure out where to place it for optimal execution.

Futures

A **future** represents a value that will eventually be available after a task completes. This is crucial when you need to perform multiple operations concurrently and then collect the results later.

```
fn        process_data_parallel(data:
List[Int]) -> List[Int]:
    let futures = map(data, fn(x):
task(fn(): Int: x * 2))
    return await futures   # Blocks
until all tasks are done
```

Here, `futures` are collected from each task, and `await` waits for all tasks to finish before proceeding. Mojo makes it easy to mix synchronous and asynchronous code while managing parallelism automatically.

Mojo's Memory Model with Concurrency

One of the common pitfalls with concurrency is managing **shared state** between tasks. Mojo ensures that when you're working with mutable state, you're not inadvertently creating race conditions.

Mojo does this by:

- **Ensuring thread safety** for shared mutable data through built-in mechanisms
- **Immutability by default** for data shared across threads

Advanced Parallel Execution Techniques

Now that you understand the basics of parallel tasks, let's look at some more advanced techniques that Mojo offers for optimizing concurrency in AI applications.

Parallelizing Loops

Often, AI computations boil down to iterating over large datasets or matrices. Mojo makes it easy to parallelize loops:

```
fn   process_large_dataset(dataset:
List[Int]):
     return     parallel_for(dataset,
fn(item): item * 2)  # Processes each
item in parallel
```

Here, `parallel_for` ensures each loop iteration runs in parallel, making it ideal for operations like matrix multiplication or processing large datasets in AI.

Task Dependencies and Synchronization

Sometimes, tasks depend on one another. Mojo provides tools to manage task dependencies and synchronization cleanly.

```
fn compute():
     let task1 = task(fn(): Int: 5 * 2)
# Task 1
```

```
    let task2 = task(fn(): Int: 3 + 4)
# Task 2
    let result = await task1  # Wait
for Task 1
    let final_result = result + await
task2  # Wait for Task 2
    return final_result
```

Here, tasks `task1` and `task2` run concurrently, but `task2` waits on `task1` to finish before performing its operation.

Scaling with Distributed Systems

In addition to **multicore parallelism**, Mojo can also scale tasks across **multiple machines** using distributed computing. You can define tasks that are distributed to nodes in a cluster, allowing you to leverage distributed systems for extremely large datasets.

For example:

```
fn    distributed_computation(data:
List[Int]):
    let           task           =
distributed_task(fn(x): x * 2, data)
```

```
return await task
```

This would send the task across nodes in a distributed setup, automatically managing task distribution and synchronization.

Debugging and Profiling Parallel Code

Parallel programming often comes with its own set of debugging and performance challenges. Mojo makes it easy to debug and profile your parallel tasks.

Debugging

Use Mojo's built-in debugging tools to track task execution:

```
debug("Task started", task_name)
```

Mojo's runtime provides detailed logs that show where and when tasks are being scheduled and executed, helping you diagnose performance bottlenecks and concurrency issues.

Profiling

To profile your parallel code, Mojo integrates with existing profiling tools such as:

- `gprof`
- `perf`
- Mojo-native tools for analyzing parallel task distribution

These tools allow you to identify where the most time is being spent and optimize your parallel execution strategy.

Synchronization and Locks

When you have multiple tasks running in parallel, there's always the potential for them to interfere with each other, especially if they are modifying shared resources. **Synchronization** ensures that tasks access shared data in a safe and predictable manner, while **locks** are tools you can use to enforce that synchronization.

Why Synchronization Matters

When two or more tasks try to access the same data simultaneously, **race conditions** can occur. For example, imagine two threads trying to update the same counter:

```
var counter: Int = 0
```

```
fn increment_counter():
    counter += 1
```

If two tasks call `increment_counter` at the same time, both may read the value of `counter` as `0`, increment it, and store it back as `1`, even though it should have been `2`. This is a **race condition**.

To solve this, we need **synchronization mechanisms** like **locks** that prevent simultaneous access to the shared resource.

Using Locks in Mojo

Mojo provides lock-based synchronization through **mutexes (mutual exclusion)**. A lock ensures that only one task can access a piece of data at a time, preventing race conditions.

Here's an example of using a lock to synchronize access to a shared resource:

```
import threading

var lock: Lock = Lock()  # Create a
lock
fn safe_increment_counter():
    lock.acquire()  # Lock access
    counter += 1
    lock.release()  # Unlock after
modifying the counter
```

In the code above:

- `lock.acquire()` locks the mutex, ensuring that no other task can access the critical section of code.
- `lock.release()` releases the lock once the task is done, allowing other tasks to acquire it.

Deadlocks and Avoiding Them

While locks prevent race conditions, **deadlocks** can occur if multiple tasks are waiting for each other's locks. A deadlock happens when two tasks hold a lock that the other task needs to proceed, leading to a situation where neither can move forward.

To avoid deadlocks, follow these best practices:

- Always acquire locks in the same order to prevent circular dependencies.
- Use **try-locks** or **timeout-based locks** to avoid waiting forever.
- Be mindful of how many locks you acquire in a single task.

```
# Example: try-lock with timeout
if lock.try_acquire(timeout=100ms):
    counter += 1
    lock.release()
else:
    print("Lock acquisition timed
out")
```

This approach helps prevent a task from waiting indefinitely for a lock.

Performance Tuning Tips

Once you understand the basics of parallelism and synchronization, the next step is **optimizing** for performance. Even in a language like Mojo, where parallelism is built-in, there are key techniques that can help you achieve better performance when scaling up your applications.

1. Minimize Lock Contention

While locks are essential for thread safety, they can become a bottleneck if too many tasks need to access the same lock at once. Here are a few strategies to reduce lock contention:

- **Use fine-grained locks**: Instead of locking the entire resource, lock smaller, more specific parts. This allows more tasks to work concurrently without waiting for a lock on the entire resource.

```
# Locking smaller sections rather
than the entire resource
fn update_user_data(user_id: Int):
    let lock =
get_lock_for_user(user_id)
    lock.acquire()
    # Update user data here
    lock.release()
```

- **Lock-free algorithms**: If your data structure allows it, you can design it to avoid locks altogether, often by using atomic operations or other lock-free techniques.

2. Optimize Task Granularity

The size of the tasks you parallelize has a direct impact on performance. If tasks are too small, the overhead of managing threads can outweigh the benefits of parallelism. On the other hand, if tasks are too large, you might not be taking full advantage of all available CPU cores.

- **Find the right balance**: Aim for tasks that are large enough to benefit from parallelism but small enough to minimize overhead. You can experiment with dividing your tasks into different sizes and benchmark the results to find the optimal granularity for your workload.

```
# Breaking a large task into smaller
parallel tasks
fn process_data_in_chunks(data:
List[Int], chunk_size: Int):
    let chunks = split(data,
chunk_size)
    let futures = map(chunks,
fn(chunk):
        task(fn(): List[Int]:
process_chunk(chunk))
    )
    return await futures
```

3. Reduce Task Creation Overhead

Task creation and management can introduce overhead, especially if tasks are small and created frequently. Mojo's task system abstracts a lot of

this, but there's still overhead in managing tasks
and switching contexts.

- **Reuse tasks**: Instead of creating a new task
  each time, consider reusing task pools for
  frequently invoked tasks. Mojo supports
  this via task queues and async task pools.

```
var task_pool = TaskPool(max_size=8)
fn process_batch(data: List[Int]):
    task_pool.enqueue(fn():
        process_data(data)
    )
```

This approach helps manage and control the
number of concurrent tasks running in your
application, reducing overhead.

4. Minimize Synchronization Overhead

When multiple tasks share resources,
synchronization mechanisms like locks can become
performance bottlenecks if overused. Use the **least
amount of synchronization necessary** and try to
avoid locks for simple operations.

- **Batch updates**: Instead of locking for each small update, batch them together and update the resource at once. This minimizes the number of lock acquisitions.

- **Immutable data structures**: When possible, prefer immutable data structures. Tasks don't need to worry about locking resources when they only work on unchangeable data.

5. Profile and Tune Memory Usage

Parallel programs often face bottlenecks not just in CPU usage, but in memory bandwidth and cache access. Mojo makes it easy to profile memory usage, so make sure you:

- **Profile memory access patterns** using tools like `perf` to identify cache misses and unnecessary memory access.

- **Optimize memory access locality** by organizing your data so that frequently accessed data is placed next to each other in memory.

```
# Example: Accessing memory in
contiguous chunks improves cache
locality
fn process_matrix_in_blocks(matrix:
Matrix):
    for block in matrix.blocks:
        process_block(block)
```

Chapter Seven

Mojo and Python Interoperability

One of Mojo's key strengths is its ability to **interoperate with Python**, allowing developers to use Mojo in existing Python-based workflows. Python has a vast ecosystem of libraries that are crucial for fields like data science, machine learning, and AI. Mojo enhances Python's capabilities by providing high-performance parallelism, lower-level memory control, and better concurrency models. In this chapter, we'll look at how you can interface Mojo with Python libraries like **NumPy**, **Pandas**, and **PyTorch**.

Interfacing with Python Libraries

Mojo offers a simple yet powerful way to call Python code directly within Mojo programs. This interoperability makes it easy to integrate Python libraries without losing the performance benefits of Mojo.

Importing Python Modules into Mojo

To use Python libraries in Mojo, you simply import them in a way similar to Python itself. Mojo's runtime handles the necessary bindings and ensures smooth interaction.

```
import python


# Calling Python code directly from
Mojo
let np = python.import('numpy')
let array = np.array([1, 2, 3, 4])
print(array)  # Output: [1 2 3 4]
```

This example demonstrates how you can call Python's numpy module directly in Mojo. The Mojo runtime ensures that Python code is executed within the Mojo environment, allowing seamless integration between both languages.

Calling NumPy from Mojo

NumPy is one of the most popular libraries for numerical computing in Python, and it's frequently used in data science and AI applications. Let's see how we can use NumPy directly in Mojo for matrix operations, as these are crucial for AI tasks like training machine learning models or processing large datasets.

Example: Using NumPy for Array Operations

```
import python

# Import NumPy
let np = python.import('numpy')

# Create a NumPy array and perform
operations
let array = np.array([1, 2, 3, 4, 5])
let result = np.sum(array)   # Sum of
the array
print(result)   # Output: 15
```

In this example, we import NumPy and use it to sum the elements of an array. Thanks to Mojo's efficient handling of Python modules, this computation will run as fast as the Python equivalent.

Using NumPy for Matrix Operations

```
let matrix_a = np.array([[1, 2], [3,
4]])
let matrix_b = np.array([[5, 6], [7,
8]])

# Matrix multiplication
let result_matrix = np.dot(matrix_a,
matrix_b)
print(result_matrix)   #   Output:
[[19 22] [43 50]]
```

Here, we perform matrix multiplication using NumPy's dot function, which is heavily optimized for speed. The ability to call this directly from Mojo provides an efficient way to integrate high-performance numerical computation into your workflows.

Calling Pandas from Mojo

Pandas is the go-to library for data manipulation and analysis in Python. It's widely used in data science, especially for handling structured data like

CSV files, SQL tables, and time-series data. Mojo can interact with Pandas DataFrames directly, giving you access to the powerful data manipulation capabilities of Pandas while benefiting from Mojo's performance optimizations.

Example: Using Pandas DataFrames

```
import python

# Importing pandas
let pd = python.import('pandas')

# Create a Pandas DataFrame
let data = pd.DataFrame({
    'name':    ['Alice',    'Bob',
'Charlie'],
    'age': [25, 30, 35]
})


print(data)
```

This simple code snippet demonstrates how to create a DataFrame using Pandas in Mojo. You can leverage all of Pandas' functions for filtering, grouping, and summarizing data, while Mojo ensures the performance benefits of parallelism and memory management.

Example: Filtering Data with Pandas

```
# Filter data based on a condition
let filtered_data = data[data['age']
> 30]
print(filtered_data)
```

Here, we filter the DataFrame to show only the rows where the age is greater than 30. By combining the ease of Pandas with Mojo's parallelism and performance, this can be done very efficiently even for large datasets.

Calling PyTorch from Mojo

PyTorch is one of the most widely used libraries for machine learning and deep learning. It provides support for tensors, neural networks, and GPU-accelerated computation. Mojo's interoperability with PyTorch allows you to leverage its powerful machine learning functionality while benefiting from Mojo's enhanced concurrency and performance.

Example: Using PyTorch with Mojo

```
import python

# Importing PyTorch
let torch = python.import('torch')

# Create a PyTorch tensor
let tensor = torch.tensor([1.0, 2.0,
3.0, 4.0])
print(tensor)
```

Here, we create a simple 1D tensor in PyTorch, which can then be used for operations like matrix multiplication or neural network training.

Example: Performing Operations with PyTorch Tensors

```
# Perform element-wise addition
let tensor_a = torch.tensor([1.0,
2.0, 3.0])
```

```
let tensor_b = torch.tensor([4.0,
5.0, 6.0])
let result_tensor = tensor_a +
tensor_b
print(result_tensor)  # Output:
[5.0, 7.0, 9.0]
```

In this example, we perform element-wise addition between two tensors. With Mojo's ability to call Python directly, you can perform sophisticated deep learning operations with minimal overhead, combining the best of both Mojo and PyTorch.

Optimizing Python Interoperability

While Mojo allows you to integrate Python libraries seamlessly, there are a few things to keep in mind when optimizing performance:

1. Minimize Cross-Language Calls

Every time you call a Python function from Mojo, there's a slight overhead in transferring data between Mojo and Python. If possible, minimize the number of times you call Python code, and try to perform as much computation as possible within Mojo itself.

For example, avoid calling Python for each element in a loop; instead, try to batch operations in Mojo and then call Python for the heavy lifting when necessary.

2. Use Mojo's Parallelism for Python-Heavy Workloads

For computationally intensive Python tasks (like matrix operations in NumPy or tensor calculations in PyTorch), use Mojo's parallelism model to distribute work across multiple threads or cores. This can significantly speed up the overall performance, especially for large datasets or deep learning tasks.

3. Avoid Excessive Memory Copies

When transferring large datasets between Mojo and Python, try to minimize unnecessary memory copies. Mojo's memory model allows you to control when and how memory is allocated, so you can ensure that data is passed between Mojo and Python efficiently.

Understanding Data Transfer Between Mojo and Python

In Mojo, you can import and call Python code seamlessly, but when working with large amounts of data, the process of transferring data from Mojo to Python (or vice versa) must be handled efficiently. Mojo's runtime handles this by providing native bindings that allow Mojo to access Python objects directly and vice versa. However, understanding how data is transferred and managed can help you avoid unnecessary overhead and bottlenecks.

Basic Data Passing: Mojo to Python

To pass data from Mojo to Python, you can create Mojo variables and use Mojo's Python runtime integration to pass them to Python. This is simple for basic types such as integers, floats, and strings.

Mojo automatically converts these basic types into their Python counterparts.

Here's an example:

```
import python

# Create a Mojo variable
let num = 42

# Pass it to Python
let result = python.eval("x = {}".format(num))
print(result)
```

In this example, Mojo creates a variable `num` and then formats it into a string for Python to evaluate. This approach works well for small data types like numbers or strings.

Passing Complex Data Structures: Lists, Arrays, and Dictionaries

When dealing with more complex data structures like **lists**, **arrays**, or **dictionaries**, passing data between Mojo and Python requires a bit more attention to detail. Mojo uses its runtime system to transfer data, but the process can involve copying data, which may not be as efficient as desired.

Here's how you can pass more complex structures:

Passing Lists Between Mojo and Python

```
import python

# Create a list in Mojo
let mojo_list = [1, 2, 3, 4, 5]

# Pass it to Python
let py_list = python.eval("mojo_list
= {}".format(mojo_list))

# Operate on the list in Python
let             result             =
python.eval("sum(mojo_list)")
print(result)  # Output: 15
```

In this example, the list is formatted as a Python list before passing it to Python. Once passed, you can operate on it just as you would with any normal Python list.

Passing NumPy Arrays Between Mojo and Python

For numerical data, **NumPy arrays** are a common structure. Mojo can work with Python's `numpy` module to create and manipulate arrays. The data transfer between Mojo and NumPy can be optimized by directly passing the array using Mojo's native bindings for NumPy.

```
import python

# Import NumPy in Python
let np = python.import('numpy')

# Create a NumPy array from Mojo data
let array = np.array([1.0, 2.0, 3.0])

# Pass it to Python
let            result            =
python.eval("np.sum(mojo_array)")
print(result)   # Output: 6.0
```

Here, Mojo creates a NumPy array by calling Python directly through Mojo's interface. This direct interaction helps prevent unnecessary data copying and allows efficient handling of large numerical datasets.

Passing Dictionaries Between Mojo and Python

Dictionaries are another widely used structure, especially for key-value pairs. Passing a dictionary from Mojo to Python can be done similarly to lists, but you need to ensure that the structure of the dictionary is consistent between the two languages.

```
import python


# Create a Mojo dictionary
let mojo_dict = {'key1': 100, 'key2':
200, 'key3': 300}


# Pass it to Python
let py_dict = python.eval("mojo_dict
= {}".format(mojo_dict))


# Operate on the dictionary in Python
let            result            =
python.eval("sum(mojo_dict.values(
))")
print(result)   # Output: 600
```

The process is essentially the same as passing lists or arrays, with the added benefit that Mojo and Python both natively support dictionaries, making the interaction smoother.

Optimizing Data Transfer: Minimizing Copies

While transferring simple data types between Mojo and Python is relatively fast, transferring complex structures (especially large datasets) can lead to significant overhead. Copying large arrays or datasets between the two languages might not be the most efficient way to exchange data.

Avoiding Unnecessary Copies

To avoid excessive copying, you can work with **shared memory** between Mojo and Python. This allows both languages to access the same data without having to create separate copies. While Mojo's Python runtime can handle some of this behind the scenes, you can take more control over memory management using shared memory techniques.

Shared Memory Example with NumPy

```
import python


# Create a NumPy array in Python
let np = python.import('numpy')
```

```
# Create a shared memory array in Mojo
let shared_array = np.zeros(1000)

# Pass shared memory between Mojo and
Python
let result =
python.eval("np.sum(shared_array)"
)
print(result)
```

In this case, Mojo directly creates a shared memory array with NumPy, which minimizes the overhead associated with copying large data structures.

Using Mojo's Async Features for Data Transfer

When working with very large datasets, especially in machine learning or AI applications, you might want to perform asynchronous operations for better throughput. Mojo's parallelism and concurrency features can be leveraged here to allow you to process multiple data transfers in parallel.

```
import python

# Create a Mojo list
let mojo_list = [1, 2, 3, 4, 5]

# Perform parallel data transfer
async fn transfer_data():
    let     result     =     await
python.eval("sum({})".format(mojo_
list))
    print(result)    # Output: 15

await transfer_data()
```

By using `async` and `await`, you can handle large data transfers without blocking the rest of your program. This approach is useful for applications where you need to pass large amounts of data without stalling execution.

Common Pitfalls and How to Avoid Them

1. **Excessive Memory Copies**: As we've discussed, copying large data structures between Mojo and Python can result in

performance bottlenecks. Always try to minimize data copying by leveraging shared memory or minimizing the number of transfers.

2. **Data Format Mismatches**: Make sure the data formats between Mojo and Python are compatible. For example, ensure that lists, dictionaries, and arrays are properly converted to the corresponding types in Python to avoid errors and unnecessary overhead.

3. **Blocking Data Transfer**: Be cautious when transferring large datasets synchronously, as it can block your program's execution. Use Mojo's async capabilities to keep the program responsive, especially when handling data-intensive tasks.

Chapter Eight

Building AI Models with Mojo

Mojo is not only designed for general-purpose high-performance programming but also aims to excel in the AI and machine learning space. The language's speed, memory management, and concurrency features make it an ideal choice for AI workloads. In this chapter, we'll guide you through the process of building machine learning models using Mojo, and explore how Mojo's advanced features can optimize AI tasks.

Using Mojo to Accelerate ML Workloads

Machine learning workloads, such as training models, manipulating data, and running inference, require high computational power, especially when working with large datasets. Mojo's ability to interface with Python libraries, combined with its built-in parallel execution model, allows developers to accelerate these workloads efficiently.

Accelerating ML Models

One of the key advantages of Mojo is that it supports **parallel execution** natively, which helps speed up tasks like training large AI models, especially when working with deep learning frameworks like **PyTorch** and **TensorFlow**. Mojo provides seamless integration with Python libraries but also allows you to run data-intensive computations directly in Mojo for even faster execution.

Here's an example of **parallelizing ML computations** with Mojo's built-in features:

```
import python


# Importing PyTorch for AI model
operations
let torch = python.import('torch')


# Create a PyTorch tensor for data
let tensor = torch.randn(10000,
10000)
```

```
# Parallelize matrix operations in
Mojo
let result = tensor @ tensor #
Matrix multiplication
```

```
# Print the result
print(result)
```

In this example, Mojo takes advantage of parallel computation to speed up matrix multiplication. The integration with PyTorch means you can use existing Python-based models and accelerate them using Mojo's concurrency features.

Data Structures for Tensors and Matrices

A crucial part of building AI models, particularly in deep learning, is dealing with **tensors** and **matrices**. These are the building blocks of neural networks and most other AI models.

Tensors in Mojo

Tensors are multi-dimensional arrays, and they're at the heart of almost every AI framework, including PyTorch and TensorFlow. Mojo simplifies working with tensors, and can integrate with existing Python tensor libraries, or even define its own optimized tensor structures for high-performance computation.

```
import python

# Importing NumPy to work with arrays
let np = python.import('numpy')

# Creating a NumPy array (tensor)
let tensor = np.random.randn(100, 100)

# Perform operations on the tensor
let sum_result = np.sum(tensor)
print(sum_result)
```

In this example, we use **NumPy** to create a tensor (which is essentially a multi-dimensional array). Mojo's seamless integration with NumPy allows you to work with large data arrays and perform computationally intensive operations in parallel, which speeds up your machine learning tasks.

Matrices in Mojo

Mojo also handles **matrices** effectively. These are essentially two-dimensional arrays and are widely used in linear algebra, which is the foundation of machine learning algorithms.

```
# Create a 2D matrix in Mojo
let matrix_a = [[1, 2, 3], [4, 5, 6]]
let matrix_b = [[7, 8, 9], [10, 11, 12]]


# Matrix multiplication (element-wise)
let result = matrix_a @ matrix_b
print(result)
```

In this example, Mojo handles **matrix multiplication** and provides a concise syntax for linear algebra operations, which are key to many ML algorithms.

Building a Simple Neural Network

Now that we've discussed the basics of handling tensors and matrices, let's dive into building a simple **neural network**. Neural networks are one of the most powerful tools for AI, and Mojo makes it easy to build them while benefiting from its performance optimizations.

Example: Simple Neural Network in Mojo

Let's build a basic neural network that performs a classification task. We'll implement a basic feedforward neural network with one hidden layer. This network will take input features, pass them through the layers, and output predictions.

```
import python


# Importing PyTorch for neural
network functionalities
let torch = python.import('torch')
let nn = python.import('torch.nn')


# Create a simple neural network
model
class SimpleNN(nn.Module):
    fn __init__(self):
        super().__init__()
```

```
        self.fc1 = nn.Linear(10, 20)
# Input layer (10 nodes) to hidden
layer (20 nodes)
        self.fc2 = nn.Linear(20, 1)
# Hidden layer (20 nodes) to output
layer (1 node)

    fn forward(self, x):
        x = self.fc1(x)  # Apply
first layer
        x = torch.relu(x)  # Apply
ReLU activation
        x = self.fc2(x)  # Apply
second layer
        return x


# Instantiate the model
let model = SimpleNN()

# Define a random input tensor
let input = torch.randn(10)  # A
random tensor of size 10 (features)

# Get the model's prediction
let prediction = model(input)
```

```
print(prediction)
```

In this example, we used **PyTorch** to define a simple feedforward neural network with one hidden layer. This network is designed to take **10 features** as input and output a single prediction. The `ReLU` activation function is applied after the first layer to introduce non-linearity.

You can extend this example to more layers, different activation functions, and other neural network architectures (e.g., convolutional or recurrent networks).

Performance Benchmarking

Benchmarking is crucial when optimizing AI models for performance. You want to make sure that your models are running as efficiently as possible. Mojo offers several ways to benchmark the performance of your machine learning models, including time measurement and parallel computation evaluation.

Measuring Execution Time

One simple way to benchmark is to measure the time it takes to perform specific operations in Mojo. Here's an example of measuring the time it takes to train a neural network:

```
import time
import python

# Import PyTorch
let torch = python.import('torch')

# Define a dummy neural network
let model = SimpleNN()

# Define input data and labels
let input = torch.randn(64, 10)   #
Batch size of 64, 10 features
let labels = torch.randn(64, 1)   #
Corresponding labels

# Start timing
let start_time = time.time()
```

```python
# Training step (forward pass)
let predictions = model(input)
let loss =
torch.nn.MSELoss()(predictions,
labels)

# Backward pass and optimization
loss.backward()

# End timing
let end_time = time.time()

# Print the time taken
let elapsed_time = end_time -
start_time
print(f"Training Time:
{elapsed_time} seconds")
```

In this example, we use **Python's `time` module** to measure the execution time of a simple forward pass and backward pass (training step) for a neural network. This helps you understand how long the operation takes, which is essential for optimizing model performance.

Benchmarking Parallelism

You can also benchmark how well Mojo handles parallelism when running ML workloads. For example, if you're training a model with a large dataset, you can measure the performance difference when using Mojo's parallel execution model.

```
import python


# Parallelized training with Mojo
async fn parallel_training():
    let input = torch.randn(10000,
10)  # Large input dataset
    let labels = torch.randn(10000,
1)  # Labels for the dataset


    # Run training in parallel
    let   predictions   =   await
model(input)
    let loss =
torch.nn.MSELoss()(predictions,
labels)
    await loss.backward()
```

```
await parallel_training()
```

Here, we parallelize the model's forward and backward passes to take advantage of multiple CPU cores. This is especially useful when dealing with large datasets and computationally intensive models.

Chapter Nine

Integrating Mojo with ML Frameworks

One of the most powerful aspects of Mojo is its ability to integrate with leading machine learning frameworks. While Mojo provides its own high-performance tools and abstractions for building AI models, it also allows you to work with the frameworks you know and love—like **TensorFlow** and **PyTorch**—to enhance your machine learning workflow. This chapter will explore how to integrate Mojo with these popular ML libraries, create custom operations and kernels, and accelerate **inference**.

Mojo with TensorFlow and PyTorch

TensorFlow and PyTorch are two of the most widely used libraries in machine learning, particularly for building neural networks. Mojo has the ability to interface with these libraries, allowing you to leverage their capabilities while benefiting from Mojo's performance optimizations.

Integrating Mojo with PyTorch

Mojo's native ability to work with **PyTorch** makes it easy to use PyTorch's extensive ecosystem of neural network modules and models, while simultaneously taking advantage of Mojo's **parallel execution** and **performance tuning** features.

Example: Using PyTorch with Mojo

In this example, we'll load a pre-trained PyTorch model and run inference on it, taking advantage of Mojo's optimizations for parallelism:

```
import python


# Importing PyTorch
let torch = python.import('torch')


# Load a pre-trained model (e.g.,
ResNet)
let model =
torch.hub.load('pytorch/vision',
'resnet18', pretrained=True)


# Put the model in evaluation mode
model.eval()
```

```
# Prepare a sample input tensor (e.g.,
an image)
let input = torch.randn(1, 3, 224,
224)  # Batch size of 1, 3 channels
(RGB), 224x224 image size

# Run inference
let output = model(input)

# Print the output
print(output)
```

In this example, Mojo runs a **ResNet** model from PyTorch, performs inference on a dummy input tensor (which could represent an image), and prints the model's predictions. By utilizing Mojo's parallel execution model, you can potentially speed up this process for larger datasets or more complex models.

Integrating Mojo with TensorFlow

Similar to PyTorch, Mojo can also interface with **TensorFlow** for machine learning tasks. TensorFlow provides a rich ecosystem for building AI models, and Mojo's ability to accelerate these models makes it an ideal choice for performance-critical applications.

Example: Using TensorFlow with Mojo

Here's an example of how to use **TensorFlow** with Mojo to run inference on a pre-trained model:

```
import python


# Importing TensorFlow
let tf = python.import('tensorflow')


# Load a pre-trained TensorFlow model
(e.g., MobileNet)
let model =
tf.keras.applications.MobileNetV2(
weights='imagenet')


# Prepare a sample input tensor (e.g.,
an image)
let input = tf.random.normal([1, 224,
224, 3])  # Batch size of 1, 224x224
image size, 3 channels (RGB)


# Run inference
```

```
let output = model(input)

# Print the output
print(output)
```

In this example, we use **TensorFlow** to load a pre-trained **MobileNetV2** model, run inference on a dummy image tensor, and print the results. Mojo accelerates the execution of this process through its **parallel execution** and **performance optimizations**.

Custom Operators and Kernels in Mojo

While Mojo provides built-in functionality for working with machine learning frameworks like PyTorch and TensorFlow, sometimes you need to implement your own **custom operators** or **kernels**. Custom operators are essential when you need to implement specific mathematical functions that are not readily available in the framework, or when you want to optimize existing operations for performance.

Creating Custom Operators

Let's say you want to implement a custom **activation function** for your neural network that is not available in TensorFlow or PyTorch. Mojo allows you to implement this function in a way that integrates seamlessly with these frameworks.

Example: Custom Activation Function in Mojo

Here's how you can define a custom **activation function** in Mojo, optimize it, and integrate it into a PyTorch-based model:

```
import python


# Custom activation function in Mojo
fn custom_activation(x: Tensor) ->
Tensor:
    return x * x   # Simple square
activation function


# Integrating with PyTorch
let torch = python.import('torch')


# Define a simple model with the custom
activation
```

```
class CustomNN(torch.nn.Module):
    fn __init__(self):
        super().__init__()
        self.fc = torch.nn.Linear(10,
5)

    fn forward(self, x):
        x = self.fc(x)
        x = custom_activation(x)    #
Apply custom activation
        return x


# Instantiate the model
let model = CustomNN()


# Create a random input tensor
let input = torch.randn(64, 10)   #
Batch size of 64, 10 features


# Run the model with custom activation
let output = model(input)
print(output)
```
In this example, we define a simple **custom activation function** that squares the input tensor.

Then, we integrate it into a simple **PyTorch neural network** model. By using Mojo's **custom functions**, you can extend PyTorch (or TensorFlow) with your own high-performance operations.

Creating Custom Kernels

In Mojo, you can also create **custom kernels** for operations like matrix multiplication, convolutions, or other operations that need to be optimized for your specific hardware. This gives you fine-grained control over how the computation is performed and ensures that you are getting the best performance for your specific application.

Case Study: Accelerating Inference

To understand the real power of Mojo in machine learning, let's look at a **case study** where we accelerate the **inference phase** of a machine learning model.

Scenario: Accelerating Inference for a Large Image Dataset

Let's say you have a deep learning model for image classification, and you need to process a large batch of images (e.g., 1,000 images) in a short amount of time. This is a typical **inference** scenario. You can use Mojo to speed up the process by taking advantage of its **parallel execution** and **memory optimizations**.

Case Study Example

```
import python

# Importing PyTorch
let torch = python.import('torch')

# Load a pre-trained model
let            model            =
torch.hub.load('pytorch/vision',
'resnet18', pretrained=True)

# Set the model to evaluation mode
model.eval()

# Prepare a batch of images (1,000
images, 224x224 size)
```

```
let batch_input = torch.randn(1000,
3, 224, 224)  # 1000 images, 3 color
channels, 224x224 resolution

# Run inference in parallel (using
Mojo's parallel execution model)
let output = model(batch_input)

# Print the output
print(output)
```

In this case study, we load a **ResNet18** model, prepare a batch of **1,000 images**, and run inference on them using Mojo. Mojo's **parallel execution** model ensures that the inference task is spread across multiple CPU cores, making the process significantly faster.

Benchmarking Results

To compare the performance of running inference on a large batch of images, we can benchmark the execution time:

```
import time

# Start the timer
let start_time = time.time()
```

```
# Run inference
let output = model(batch_input)

# End the timer
let end_time = time.time()

# Calculate the elapsed time
let elapsed_time = end_time -
start_time
print(f"Inference Time for 1000
Images: {elapsed_time} seconds")
```

By leveraging Mojo's parallel processing and memory management capabilities, we can achieve a significant speedup in inference time, particularly for large datasets like this one. Benchmarking helps us track the performance improvements and confirm that Mojo is delivering faster results.

Chapter Ten

Metaprogramming in Mojo

Compile-Time Execution

In Mojo, **compile-time execution** allows you to run code during the compilation process. This can significantly reduce runtime overhead by precomputing values or logic during compilation. Compile-time execution is particularly useful for optimizations, code generation, and ensuring that certain logic is validated before the program runs.

Example: Compile-Time Constant Folding

In Mojo, you can perform certain calculations during compile time. For instance, if you know a constant value at compile time, you can use it directly in your code without needing to perform the computation at runtime. This feature can save valuable processing time in performance-critical applications.

```
// Define a constant expression
```

```
let pi = 3.14159

// Compute the area of a circle at
compile time
let radius = 5
let area = pi * radius * radius

// The calculation happens at compile
time, so it's fast at runtime
print("Area of Circle: ", area)
```
Here, the calculation for the **area of the circle** is precomputed during compilation, meaning that no unnecessary computation happens when the program is executed.

Example: Compile-Time Type Checking

Mojo also allows you to check types at compile time to ensure that your program is more robust. If a function is expecting a specific type, Mojo will ensure that the types are correct at compile time rather than allowing runtime errors.

```
// Compile-time type checking
```

```
fn calculate_area(radius: i32) ->
i32:
    return 3 * radius * radius

// Correct usage
let area = calculate_area(5)  //
This will compile

// Incorrect usage - compile-time
error
let area = calculate_area("five")
// Compile-time error: expected i32
```

In this case, Mojo enforces type safety during compilation, preventing the error before the program ever runs.

Type-Level Programming

Type-level programming allows developers to write programs where the types of data can be manipulated or used to infer certain behaviors, enabling powerful abstractions and optimizations.

Mojo offers rich **type-level programming** features, enabling you to encode logic into types.

Example: Type-Level Calculations

Let's say you want to encode constraints based on types. For example, you could create a **type class** that only accepts numbers that are powers of 2, ensuring that your program works only with valid types at compile time.

```
// Type-level programming example
fn is_power_of_two(x: i32) -> bool:
    return (x & (x - 1)) == 0  //
Bitwise check for powers of two


// Using type-based constraints
let num = 8

if is_power_of_two(num):
    print(f"{num} is a power of 2")
else:
    print(f"{num} is not a power of
2")
```

Here, **type-level logic** ensures that only numbers that meet specific criteria (powers of two) are processed, allowing you to build more efficient, safer programs.

Macros and Code Generation

Macros and **code generation** are key components of metaprogramming. With macros, you can generate code dynamically based on the structure of your program. This allows you to automate repetitive tasks or introduce new patterns that would otherwise require a lot of manual coding. In Mojo, macros operate at compile time, generating optimized code as needed.

Example: Defining a Simple Macro

A basic example of a macro is one that generates a function for repetitive operations, such as logging.

```
// Define a macro to generate logging
functions
macro    log_function(name:    str,
message: str):
```

```
fn name():
    print(message)
```

```
// Using the macro to create specific
log functions
log_function(info_log, "This is an
info log")
log_function(warning_log, "This is a
warning log")
```

```
// Call generated functions
info_log()  // Output: This is an
info log
warning_log()  // Output: This is a
warning log
```

In this example, the macro **log_function** generates multiple functions (like `info_log` and `warning_log`) that log specific messages. This can reduce redundancy and help ensure consistency across your codebase.

Example: Code Generation for Repetitive Tasks

Consider a situation where you need to generate **getter and setter functions** for a struct. Instead of writing them out manually, you can define a macro to automatically generate these functions.

```
// Macro for generating getter and
setter functions
macro generate_getter_setter(name:
str):
    fn name_getter() -> str:
        return name

    fn name_setter(new_name: str):
        name = new_name


// Use the macro to generate
functions for a struct field
generate_getter_setter(name)
```

This macro would automatically create getter and setter functions for a variable. This is incredibly useful when dealing with large data structures and wanting to maintain consistency and save time.

Benefits of Metaprogramming in Mojo

Using metaprogramming in Mojo has several key advantages:

1. **Performance Optimizations**: By moving certain computations to **compile time**, you can reduce runtime overhead and make your programs run faster. For example, performing type checks or constant folding at compile time can reduce the need for costly computations at runtime.

2. **Reusability and Abstraction**: Macros and code generation allow you to write more abstract and reusable code, reducing duplication and improving maintainability. You can generate boilerplate code on the fly, leaving you to focus on the core functionality of your application.

3. **Type Safety**: Type-level programming ensures that type constraints are respected throughout the program, preventing runtime errors and making your code safer and more predictable.

4. **Flexibility and Control**: With macros and type-level computations, Mojo gives you fine-grained control over your code. You can dynamically generate code based on various conditions, allowing for sophisticated patterns and optimizations.

Chapter Eleven

Mojo for Systems Programming

Writing High-Performance Libraries

A key use case for Mojo in systems programming is in the development of **high-performance libraries**. Whether you are writing a general-purpose library or one specialized for computational tasks like **linear algebra**, **image processing**, or **network protocols**, Mojo provides the tools necessary to ensure that your code is both efficient and optimized for modern hardware.

Example: Implementing a Fast Math Library

Let's start by considering a simple example where we write a basic math library for vector operations. Here, performance is essential because these operations are often used in computational-heavy applications like **AI**, **graphics programming**, and **game development**.

```
// High-performance vector addition
using Mojo
struct Vector:
    x: f32
    y: f32

fn add_vectors(v1: Vector, v2:
Vector) -> Vector:
    return Vector(x = v1.x + v2.x, y
= v1.y + v2.y)

// Using the vector library
let vec1 = Vector(3.0, 4.0)
let vec2 = Vector(1.0, 2.0)

let result = add_vectors(vec1, vec2)
print(f"Resulting                vector:
({result.x}, {result.y})")
```

In this example, the **vector addition function** performs the calculation efficiently. By using Mojo's optimized memory management and **low-level performance features**, you can ensure that the operations scale well for larger data sets and intensive computation.

Hardware-Level Programming and SIMD

One of Mojo's key advantages is its ability to perform **hardware-level programming**, including direct access to **SIMD** (Single Instruction, Multiple Data) operations. SIMD allows you to process multiple data points simultaneously with a single instruction, greatly improving performance for certain computational tasks, such as image processing, matrix multiplication, or any task involving large datasets.

SIMD Operations in Mojo

Mojo provides mechanisms to access and take full advantage of modern CPU features like SIMD, making it ideal for writing **high-performance computational libraries** or performing **data-parallel operations**. With SIMD, operations that can be parallelized across multiple data elements will execute faster.

For example, let's say you want to compute the **dot product** of two vectors. Instead of performing the operation sequentially, you can use SIMD to process multiple elements in parallel.

```
//    SIMD-based    dot    product
calculation in Mojo
fn dot_product_simd(v1: Vector, v2:
Vector) -> f32:
    let result = (v1.x * v2.x) + (v1.y
* v2.y)
    return result


// Calling the SIMD-optimized dot
product function
let vec1 = Vector(1.0, 2.0)
let vec2 = Vector(3.0, 4.0)


let    dot_product_result    =
dot_product_simd(vec1, vec2)
print(f"Dot    Product    Result:
{dot_product_result}")
```

In a real-world application, this function could be enhanced with **SIMD intrinsics** to ensure that the computation is offloaded to multiple cores or handled by **vectorized instructions** in the CPU. This allows for massive speedups in performance-intensive tasks.

Mojo in Embedded and Edge AI

Mojo is also an excellent choice for **embedded systems programming**, where you often deal with limited resources and need to make every cycle count. Embedded systems often require **real-time processing** and **low-power consumption**, and Mojo's high-performance nature and ability to interface with low-level hardware make it a powerful tool for these tasks.

Example: Using Mojo in Embedded Systems

Consider a scenario where you need to interface with hardware sensors in an embedded system, such as reading data from an accelerometer or temperature sensor. Mojo can directly communicate with hardware via memory-mapped I/O or device drivers.

```
// Pseudo code for reading sensor
data in Mojo (embedded systems)
```

```
fn read_sensor_data(sensor_address:
u32) -> f32:
    // Simulate reading a sensor at
a specific address
    return *sensor_address //
Dereferencing   a   memory-mapped
register

let sensor_data =
read_sensor_data(0x1000) // Read
from memory-mapped address
print(f"Sensor                Data:
{sensor_data}")
```

In this example, Mojo accesses a **memory-mapped register** to read the sensor data. You can extend this code to include real-time processing features that are critical for **IoT (Internet of Things)** and **edge AI** applications.

Edge AI with Mojo

Edge AI involves running machine learning models locally on devices (edge devices) instead of relying on cloud-based computing. This is critical for

real-time decision-making, low-latency requirements, and **offline operation** in devices like drones, autonomous vehicles, and smart cameras. Mojo can be used to **accelerate machine learning models** and run them efficiently on edge devices, leveraging both **CPU and GPU** capabilities. Mojo's ability to interact with Python libraries like **TensorFlow** or **PyTorch** makes it easy to load pre-trained models and run inferences on these devices.

Example: Deploying a Simple AI Model on an Edge Device

Let's consider an example where we deploy a **pre-trained neural network model** on an edge device. The model could be trained in Python and then run in Mojo for real-time inference.

```
import torch
import numpy as np

// Example: Run inference with a
pre-trained PyTorch model
```

```
fn run_inference(model:
torch.nn.Module, input_data:
np.ndarray) -> np.ndarray:
    let tensor_input =
torch.tensor(input_data)
        let output = model(tensor_input)
        return output.numpy()


// Run inference on an edge device
let model = torch.load("model.pth")
// Load a pre-trained model
let input_data = np.array([1.0, 2.0,
3.0, 4.0])  // Example input


let output = run_inference(model,
input_data)
print(f"Inference Result:
{output}")
```

In this example, the **PyTorch model** is loaded and inference is performed on the edge device using Mojo. By combining Mojo with AI frameworks like **PyTorch** and **TensorFlow**, you can run powerful AI models even on resource-constrained devices.

Performance Tuning for Systems Programming

When working with systems programming, performance is paramount. Mojo provides several tools to **optimize** code, especially in the context of low-level operations like **memory management**, **concurrency**, and **parallelism**.

Example: Optimizing for Cache Efficiency

In systems programming, cache performance plays a huge role in ensuring your program runs efficiently. Mojo allows you to write code that is aware of **cache locality**, minimizing cache misses and optimizing memory access patterns.

```
// Optimizing matrix multiplication
for cache locality
fn      optimized_matrix_multiply(A:
[[f32]], B: [[f32]]) -> [[f32]]:
    let n = A.size
    let result = [[f32]](n, n)   //
Initialize result matrix
```

```
// Loop with cache optimization
(e.g., blocking or tiling)
    for i in 0..<n:
        for j in 0..<n:
            let sum = 0.0
            for k in 0..<n:
                sum += A[i][k] *
B[k][j]
            result[i][j] = sum
    return result
```

Here, **loop unrolling** or **blocking techniques** could
be applied to optimize the access pattern for large
matrices, significantly improving performance in
tasks like **scientific computing**, **AI training**, and
data analytics.

Chapter Twelve

Real-World Projects and Case Studies

AI-Powered Image Recognition

Project Overview

Image recognition is foundational in many industries—healthcare, security, retail, and autonomous systems. With Mojo's **tight integration with Python** and **hardware acceleration**, you can build models that process images faster and deploy them with greater efficiency.

Tech Stack

- Mojo (for performance-critical components)
- PyTorch (for neural network modeling)
- OpenCV (for image handling)
- NumPy (for array manipulation)

Implementation Steps

1. **Image Preprocessing**
2. `import cv2`
3. `import numpy as np`
4. `fn preprocess_image(path: str)`
   `-> np.ndarray:`
5.   `let img = cv2.imread(path,`
   `cv2.IMREAD_GRAYSCALE)`
6.   `let resized =`
   `cv2.resize(img, (28, 28))  //`
   `e.g., MNIST size`
7.   `return resized / 255.0  //`
   `Normalize pixel values`
8. **Model Integration**
9. `import torch`
10. `fn run_inference(model:`
    `torch.nn.Module, input_image:`
    `np.ndarray) -> int:`
11.   `let tensor =`
    `torch.tensor(input_image).uns`
    `queeze(0).unsqueeze(0)  // Add`
    `batch & channel dims`
12.   `let output = model(tensor)`

```
13.    return
    torch.argmax(output).item()
```

14. **Use Case** Build an MNIST digit recognizer or train a custom model on a medical image dataset (e.g., for tumor detection).

Mojo for Reinforcement Learning

Project Overview

Reinforcement learning (RL) is used in **robotics, gaming, autonomous vehicles**, and **decision-making systems**. Mojo shines here by accelerating the training loop, especially when simulations are involved.

Tech Stack

- Mojo (for fast environment simulation)
- Python (for high-level orchestration)
- Gymnasium (OpenAI Gym)
- PyTorch (policy/value networks)

Key Components

1. **Simulating the Environment** Mojo can optimize the **step function** used in an RL environment:

2. ```
struct State:
```

3. ```
    position: f32
```

4. ```
    velocity: f32
```

5. ```
fn step(state: State, action: f32) -> State:
```

6. ```
    let new_position = state.position + action * 0.1
```

7. ```
    let new_velocity = 0.9 * state.velocity + action
```

8. ```
    return State(new_position, new_velocity)
```

9. **Policy Optimization** Use Mojo to write performance-tuned versions of:

   o   Reward calculation

   o   Transition simulations

   o   State evaluations

10. **Use Case** Train an agent to solve a **continuous control problem** like CartPole, LunarLander, or even a robotic arm.
```

Mojo in Finance and Predictive Analytics

Project Overview

The financial sector demands **real-time analysis**, **low-latency systems**, and **predictive accuracy**. Mojo can be used to optimize:

- Financial time series analysis
- Fraud detection
- Portfolio optimization

Example: Stock Price Predictor

1. **Preprocessing Time Series**
2. ```
   import pandas as pd
   ```
3. ```
   fn load_and_process_data(path: str) -> pd.DataFrame:
   ```
4. ```
       let df = pd.read_csv(path)
   ```
5. ```
       df["returns"] = df["Close"].pct_change()
   ```
6. ```
       return df.dropna()
   ```
7. **Predictive Model in Mojo + PyTorch**
8. ```
   import torch.nn as nn
   ```
9. ```
   class LSTMModel(nn.Module):
   ```
   ```

```
10.     def __init__(self,
   input_size, hidden_size,
   num_layers):
11.          super().__init__()
12.          self.lstm          =
   nn.LSTM(input_size,
   hidden_size,          num_layers,
   batch_first=True)
13.          self.fc            =
   nn.Linear(hidden_size, 1)
14.     def forward(self, x):
15.          out, _ = self.lstm(x)
16.          return self.fc(out[:,
   -1, :])
```

17. **Mojo Acceleration** Mojo can be used for:

- o Preprocessing input features (sliding window creation, normalization)
- o Fast streaming data ingestion
- o Real-time inference from a deployed model

Chapter Thirteen

The Future of Mojo

Mojo in Open Source and Industry

Why Open Source Matters

Mojo began as a performance-first programming language but quickly embraced the **open source model** to foster innovation, trust, and collaboration. This decision mirrors successful languages like Python, Rust, and Julia. Open sourcing Mojo ensures:

- **Transparency** in development and roadmap
- **Faster innovation** through community contributions
- **Wider adoption** across academia and industry

Industrial Use Cases

Major companies are already experimenting with Mojo in performance-critical environments. These include:

- **AI startups** building low-latency inference engines
- **Robotics companies** optimizing control loops
- **Edge computing platforms** leveraging Mojo's tight hardware integration
- **High-frequency trading firms** streamlining data throughput

If you're in a field where milliseconds matter, Mojo is not just a toy—it's a strategic tool.

The Mojo Ecosystem and Community

Ecosystem Overview

Mojo is rapidly evolving into an ecosystem rather than just a standalone language. Here's a quick snapshot of the expanding landscape:

Component	Purpose

Mojo Standard Library	Core utilities, math, data structures
MojoML	High-performance ML tooling built on Mojo
Mojo-Python Bridge	Seamless interop layer for Python
Mojo Package Manager	(In development) Dependency and build management system
Mojo VSCode Plugin	IDE support with syntax highlighting and debugging tools

The real strength of Mojo's ecosystem comes from its **composability**. You can write high-performance code in Mojo and plug it directly into Python pipelines or compile it for embedded systems.

Growing Community

- **Discord & Forums**: Fast-growing with active Q&A, code reviews, and announcements
- **GitHub Projects**: Public repositories for compiler development, libraries, and tools

- **Meetups and Conferences**: Mojo tracks are popping up in AI and systems programming conferences

As the community grows, your contributions—whether code, documentation, or tutorials—can help shape how Mojo evolves.

Contribution Guide and Resources

How to Contribute

Getting started with contributing to Mojo doesn't require deep compiler knowledge. Here are ways to make a meaningful impact:

1. **Report Bugs**
   Test Mojo thoroughly in your own projects and file detailed issues on GitHub.
2. **Write Examples and Tutorials**
   Help others learn by explaining what you already know.

3. **Improve Documentation**

    If something confused you, there's a good chance it'll confuse others. Fix it.

4. **Contribute Code**

    Whether it's a new feature, performance fix, or small utility—every line counts.

Resources to Start With

-   Mojo GitHub Repository

    Main codebase, issues, and contribution guidelines.

-   Mojo Docs

    Official documentation, examples, and language references.

-   Modular Community Forums

    Connect with developers, get feedback, and discuss roadmaps.

-   Mojo Discord

    Real-time chats, code sharing, and help channels.

Appendix A: Mojo Language Reference

This appendix serves as a **quick-reference guide** to the Mojo programming language—ideal for looking up syntax, understanding core types, and exploring what's available out-of-the-box via the standard library. Whether you're deep in a project or brushing up before an interview, this section provides concise, structured information at a glance.

Syntax Guide

Basic Structure

```
fn greet(name: String) -> None:
    print("Hello, " + name)
```

Variable Declaration

```
let x: Int = 10
var y = 20  # Inferred as Int
```

Control Flow

```
if x > 0:
```

```
    print("Positive")
elif x == 0:
    print("Zero")
else:
    print("Negative")
```

Loops

```
for i in range(0, 5):
    print(i)
while x > 0:
    x -= 1
```

Functions

```
fn add(a: Int, b: Int) -> Int:
    return a + b
```

Structs and Tuples

```
struct Point:
    x: Float
    y: Float
let p = Point(1.0, 2.0)
let pair = (3, "Mojo")  # Tuple
```

Built-in Types

Type	Description
Int	Integer (platform-sized)
Float	Floating-point number
Bool	Boolean (true or false)
String	UTF-8 encoded text
List[T]	Generic list of items of type T
Set[T]	Unordered collection of unique items
Map[K, V]	Key-value pairs
Optional[T]	Nullable type, may be None

Standard Library Overview

Module	Description
Math	Common mathematical functions/constants
Time	Time tracking and delays
Os	Filesystem and operating system interfaces
Collections	Lists, maps, sets, and related utilities

Async	Asynchronous execution and concurrency helpers
Ml	Tensors, matrices, and ML-specific structures
Ffi	Interfacing with Python and native code

Appendix B: Tools and Resources

This section includes tools and environments that enhance your Mojo development workflow, plus learning materials to grow your mastery.

Editors, Plugins, and IDEs

Visual Studio Code (Recommended)

- **Plugin**: Mojo extension from Modular
- **Features**: Syntax highlighting, linting, IntelliSense, REPL integration

Other Options

- **Neovim/Emacs**: Community-driven syntax plugins

- **JetBrains IDEs**: Mojo plugin under development

Mojo REPL and CLI

Starting the REPL

```
mojo reply
```

Use this for rapid prototyping and trying out syntax on the fly.

Common CLI Commands

Command	Description
`mojo run file.mojo`	Compile and run a Mojo file
`mojo fmt file.mojo`	Format your code
`mojo build`	Build and compile Mojo packages
`mojo test`	Run test files